ALL ABOUT ME—
A JOURNEY TO THE INSIDE

Understanding the Three-Part Nature of Man

THE WORKBOOK

Elvie Dell

"All About Me—A Journey to The Inside: The Workbook," by Elvie Dell. ISBN 978-1-62137-447-3 (Softcover)

Published 2014 by Virtualbookworm.com Publishing Inc., P.O. Box 9949, College Station, TX 77842, US.

Manufactured in the United States of America.

FOREWORD

It is a very freeing thing in the Christian walk to have an understanding of your three-part being (spirit, soul, and body) and to know what your purpose and destiny in life is. We are fearfully and wonderfully made by an amazing and creative God. Many aspects of life are multi-dimensional, so it should come as no surprise that we, being created in His image, are multi-dimensional as well.

People are often confused because they don't really understand how they are made and where their struggles really lie. Not realizing that what they go through is common to us all can cause silent suffering, isolation, and even self-condemnation. Our Father wants us to be free and to walk in peace with Him, ourselves, and others.

This workbook is designed to be used in conjunction with the original text, "All About Me--A Journey to the Inside." It can be used individually or in group settings. It is designed to be very simple so that any age level from elementary on up can grasp these truths. The main purpose for the workbook is to follow up on what you've read and ensure that "you got it."

The first portion of each workbook chapter is repetitious of the chapter readings. It's one thing to read something; it's another to have to say it back, or confirm it--thus the "Content Comprehension Questions." That's how you get it in your heart.

The second section of each workbook chapter is a "Life Application Section" which allows you to reflect on your own personal walk, encouraging you to dig deep, examine yourself, be honest with yourself, and move forward.

This book and study is designed to help lead you to a deeper understanding of yourself with the belief that increased understanding will take you to greater levels of peace, joy, and acceptance of yourself and others.

*Study questions are taken from the original text and any references are so noted in the original text.

TABLE OF CONTENTS

INTRODUCTION

Salvation itself is a spiritual conversion while sanctification is a process that follows. We walk it out in our Christian life. Understanding we are a three-part being and learning to differentiate between these different aspects helps us to realize that much of what we experience in life is normal and all a part of the human experience. It brings us to a place of peace that we may move forward in confidence and victory and fulfill our destiny in Christ.

Content Comprehension Questions
Refer back to the Introduction to answer the following questions.

1. What is a born-again Christian believer? (p. 1)

2. There is a _____ for God's people. (p. 1)

3. 2 Corinthians 5:17 tells us that if we are in Christ, we are a _____ _____. (p. 1)

4. The "new creature" 2 Corinthians 5:17 talks about is our _____ man. (p. 1)

5. We are actually a _____ part being. (p. 1-2)

6. Those parts are _____, _____, and _____. (p. 2)

7. People need to recognize where their _____ really lie and how to hear from their _____. (p. 2)

8. They need to have the assurance that God has a _____ _____ for their lives. (p. 2)

Chapter 1
WHAT'S UP WITH ME?

Even after asking Jesus into our hearts, we may not see a miraculous change in our lives right away. The following study questions will help you to understand that the road to sanctification is not a single destination, but a long and winding journey.

Content Comprehension Questions
Refer back to chapter 1 to answer the following questions.

1. We're really all very much _____ _____. (p. 8)

2. There is a _____ _____ common to us all, and it's waged _____ _____. (p. 8)

3. We all deal with _____ thoughts and _____, simply because we don't _____ ourselves and how we were _____. (p. 8)

4. You are actually a _____ part being. (p. 8)

5. Those parts are as follows:

      You ARE a _____.

      You HAVE a _____.

      You LIVE in a _____. (p. 9)

6. Your _____ is the real you, the eternal part that's like God. (p. 9)

7. Your soul deals with your _____ and your ability to _____ and _____. (p. 9)

8. Your body is simply the "_____" you live in. (p. 9)

9. Changing your life after salvation is a _____ that may take time, so it is important not to become discouraged if change does not happen right away. (p. 9

10. Understanding our _____ - _____ being is the key to walking in _____. (p. 10)

11. You are a "spiritual being having a _____ experience, rather than a human being having a _____ experience." (p. 10)

Life Application: What's Up With Me?

Use the concepts from chapter 1 to help you complete the following life application questions.

1. When did you accept Jesus as your Lord and Savior?

2. How did you do it? What were the circumstances?

3. As discussed on page 9, did you experience "miraculous deliverance" when you first accepted salvation? If so, please explain this experience. If you did NOT, please explain what DID happen.

4. How did this make you feel?

5. Make a list of ways you can better focus on the PROCESS of change:

Chapter 2
THE HIDDEN MAN OF YOUR HEART—YOUR SPIRIT

Our spirits frequently speak to us, but often through lack of knowledge or recognition we can't (or don't) listen. The following study questions will help you better identify with your spirit to enhance your understanding and responsiveness to its voice.

Content Comprehension Questions
Refer back to chapter 2 to answer the following questions.

1. You've got to get _____ to hear your spirit. This voice is not very _____. (p. 11)

2. Your spirit is actually the most _____ part of you--the part of you that's like God. (p. 11)

3. Your spirit is the part of you that got "_____ _____" at salvation. (p. 12)

4. God _____ with you through your spirit. (p. 12)

5. How do people sometimes refer to their spirit? (p. 12)

6. When your spirit prompts you to take certain actions, it will never be anything that goes against _____ _____. (p. 12)

7. What do you need to be able to do in order to recognize the truth of your spirit? (p. 12)

8. Many times, people ignore their spirit because they don't _____ it's their spirit talking to them. (p. 13)

9. The voice of your spirit often defies _____, reason, and _____. It doesn't come from your _____. It comes from a much deeper _____. (p. 14)

10. Developing a _____ to the voice of your spirit and obeying it will prove to be to your _____. (p. 15)

11. What are some things that can distract you from hearing your spirit? (p. 15)

12. Every believer has the privilege of hearing _____ _____ _____ _____ _____. (p. 16)

13. Developing your spirit takes _____ and _____. (p. 16)

14. Your spirit's "recommended diet" is: _____ (p. 16)

15. What are some ways to feed or develop your spirit? (p. 16)

16. The author recommends _____ _____ _____ as "one good way to develop your spirit." (p. 16)

17. What does Kenneth Copeland suggest to do as one of the quickest ways to learn the voice of your spirit? (p. 18)

Life Application: Your Spirit

Use the concepts from chapter 2 to help you complete the following life application questions.

1. Write down a few instances where you heard your spirit speak to you.

2. How did you know your spirit was communicating with you?

3. What was your response?

4. Have you ever heard your spirit speak to you, and you ignored it? What was the outcome?

5. How would you describe your spirit? (Use descriptive words, draw pictures, write a few lines of poetry—whatever helps you convey the image of your personal spirit.)

6. Make a list of ways you can better listen to your spirit:

7. How can you make time in your schedule to focus on your spirit?

8. Finally, how can you help others to recognize and connect with their own spirits?

Chapter 3
MR. TROUBLE—YOUR SOUL
(YOUR MIND, WILL, & EMOTIONS)

Each of us has a mind, will, and emotions that often overlap, causing turmoil for our souls. The following study questions will help you not only recognize when your soul is in turmoil, but help you to calm the chaos with God's Word.

Content Comprehension Questions: Your Soul (General)
Refer back to chapter 3 to answer the following questions.

1. Your soul houses these 3 things (p. 21):

   _____

   _____, and

   _____

2. The soul is the part that most people are _____ with. (p. 21)

3. People often mistake their soul as the "_____" them. (p. 21)

4. The _____ and soul are often thought to be the same thing. But in fact, they are _____. (p. 21-22)

5. Think of your soul as your _____, and all the energy behind it. (p. 22)

6. Your soul responds to _____ _____. (p. 22)

7. Responding to things around you according to what's going on in your mind and emotional realm, and allowing your thoughts and feelings to spur you to action, is called: _____ _____ _____ _____ _____. (p.22) This will cause you to continually be _____. (p. 22)

8. You have a _____ about your responses and your _____. (p. 23)

9. **TRUE** or **FALSE**: The different parts of your soul tend to overlap and get mixed together. (p. 23)

10. Your soul did not change when you got _____ _____. (p. 23)

11. You may still have a lot of the same _____ you had before because your soul has been trained by a _____ _____. (p. 23)

12. Without restraint, responding to your soul can lead to _____. (p. 24)

Life Application: Your Soul (General)
Use the concepts from chapter 3 to help you complete the following life application questions.

General Questions

1. Write down an instance where you have been guilty of "living out of your soul." (p. 22)

2. What were the ramifications of this?

MIND

Content Comprehension Questions: Your Mind
Refer back to chapter 3 to answer the following questions.

1. Your mind is a lot like a _____. (p. 25)

2. LOGIC lives in this part of your soul: _____ (p. 25)

3. Your mind deals with the _____ realm, or your intellect; the part of you that _____ and thinks. It houses your _____. (p. 25)

4. Your mind needs to be _____ _____ and _____ to get rid of the things that don't line up with God's Word. This is called "_____ _____ _____". (p. 25)

5. The reprogramming of your mind is _____ responsibility. You are the _____ of your own self. You have to _____ your mind, _____ your attitude, and _____ what you're thinking. (p. 26)

6. Define "mindset." (p. 26)

7. You can change a mindset on purpose, with the _____ _____ _____. (p. 26)

8. What does the author suggest to do to change your mindset? The first step is to become _____ of what's running through there all the time. (p. 27) Make the effort to become conscious of your thoughts and stay in _____ of what's going through your mind. (p. 27)

9. Things get into your mind through your _____ and your _____. (p. 27)

10. Be conscious of things that have a _____ _____ on your thoughts. (p. 28)

11. As you learn and believe the Word, you'll begin to _____ _____ which thoughts _____ _____ with the Word and which ones don't. (p. 30)

12. Knowing God's Word will enable you to _____ every thought by that standard. (p. 30)

13. If a thought doesn't line up with the Word of God, it's _____ _____ _____. (p. 20)

14. It's not a sin to have a bad or wrong thought, but don't _____ on it. Get _____ of it. (p. 30)

15. You _____ a thought by speaking it. (p. 30)

16. How do you control, or change, your thoughts? (p. 31)

    You must fight thoughts with: _____. (p. 31)

17. We tend to believe the things we think, so we need to be sure our _____ is right. (p. 33)

18. What is established in your mind will get into your _____. (p. 33)

19. You have to do more than just dismiss negative thoughts, you must _____ them. (p. 33-34)

20. When the _____ of God and the _____ of God control your mind, you will

    be filled with _____ and _____. (p. 34)

21. You conquer and gain victory over your mind, one _____ at a time. (p. 35)

22. The more you _____, the easier it becomes. (p. 35)

Life Application: Your Mind

Use the concepts from chapter 3 to help you complete the following life application questions.

Your Mind

1. Do you experience thoughts you are afraid do not align with God's Word?

2. List some ways you can work on changing your mindset to better align with God's Word:

3. How can you better handle situations in which someone has offended you? In which you experience anxiety? In which you are afraid?

4. What can you do to encourage yourself when it seems like the battle against impure thoughts seems fruitless?

EMOTIONS

Content Comprehension Questions: Your Emotions
Refer back to chapter 3 to answer the following questions.

1. Your emotions are your _____. (p. 35)

2. Emotions _____ all the time. (p. 36)

3. **TRUE** or **FALSE**: Your emotions are reliable. (p. 36)

4. Emotions simply let you _____ what you are thinking. (p. 36)

5. When people react to their emotions, they usually _____ and _____ things they later regret. (p. 36)

6. Emotions are meant to be a _____ and to enhance your life. (p. 36)

7. Write or diagram the progression from thoughts to consequences. (p. 37)

8. The emotions we experience are _____ to all people. They are JUST _____. (p. 40)

9. It takes _____ and _____ to handle our emotions. (p. 40)

Life Application: Your Emotions
Use the concepts from chapter 3 to help you complete the following life application questions.

<u>Your Emotions</u>

1. Write down an instance where you have let your emotions get the better of you.

2. Why do you think you reacted that way?

3. In the future, how can you better control your emotions?

4. How can you keep others' negative emotions from affecting your own emotions?

WILL

Content Comprehension Questions: Your Will
Refer back to chapter 3 to answer the following questions.

1. Your will plays an awesome and _____ part in your life. He carries a lot of _____ for the direction of your life. (p. 40-41)

2. God has given every man a _____will and the independence to choose his own _____. (p. 41)

3. Walking out your commitment to follow Christ is an ongoing process that is done one _____ at a time. (p. 41)

4. Great _____ comes with a free will because God holds us _____ for our choices. (p. 41)

5. God will allow you to choose your own _____. (p. 42)

6. Your will _____ whether you yield to the dictates of the spirit, the soul or the flesh. (p. 42)

7. All the "_____" of your three-part being are crying out for leadership. (p. 42)

8. To be effective for the kingdom of God, and to have victory and _____ in your life and the destiny God has planned for you, you have to make a _____ _____ of your will that you're going to follow your spirit. (p. 43)

9. This takes personal _____. (p. 44)

10. A defiant will, set against the things of God, will lead you into _____. (p. 45)

11. God wants you to willingly _____. (p. 45)

12. He wants you to serve Him because you really _____ to. (p. 45)

13. Sometimes God allows things such as negative _____, or even _____, in order to bring us to a place where we become willing. (p. 45-46)

14. Define grace. (p. 48)

15. God loves us beyond our human strength and _____. He wants us to _____ to Him for help and _____. Just as we could not _____ ourselves, so we also need him to _____ through our daily _____ with us. God is looking at our _____, and our _____ to align with His will, not our ability to accomplish it on our own. (p. 48-49)

16. Engage your will to get up and keep moving _____. His grace will cause you to _____. (p. 49)

Life Application: Your Will
Use the concepts from chapter 3 to help you complete the following life application questions.

Your Will

1. The author states that sometimes God allows negative consequences to happen to us in order to bring us to a willing place (p. 45). Have you ever experienced this? What happened?

2. Did facing negative consequences help guide you towards being willing to accept God's Word? How so?

3. Why do you think it's important to follow God's will and not our own?

4. List some ways you can practice focusing your will on God's Word:

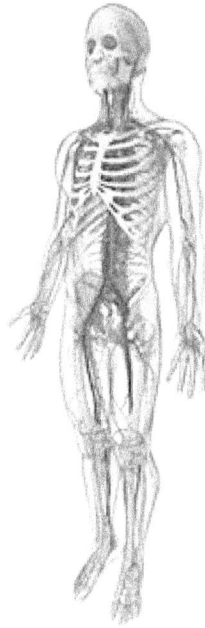

Chapter 4
MR. BIG MOUTH—YOUR BODY

Perhaps one of the biggest challenges you will face in your spiritual journey is rejecting the physical, or material, desires of your body. The following study questions will help you understand the necessary steps you must take to ensure your body does not win its battle to "be the boss."

Content Comprehension Questions
Refer back to chapter 4 to answer the following questions.

1. Your body did not _____ when you got saved. (p. 52)

2. Unless supernatural deliverance came at salvation, you still have the same _____.
   (p. 52)

3. Your body calls out for _____ things your flesh wants. (p. 52)

4. A good indicator of how spiritually strong you are is how much _____ you have over your body. (p. 53)

5. Your body is simply the place where your _____ lives. (p. 53)

6. Your body enables you to get around and have the ability to _____ with your physical environment. (p. 54)

7. _____ _____ is the leading cause of preventable morbidity and mortality in the United States. (p. 55)

8. List some ways to take care of your physical body. (p. 55)

9. List some behaviors that are destructive to your body. (p. 55)

10. **TRUE** or **FALSE**: Of all the creatures God has made, only humans have the gift of speech. (p. 57)

11. Death and life are in the power of the _____. (p. 57)

12. How should we use our words? (p. 58)

13. As well as communicating with others, God wants you to communicate with _____. List some ways to do this. (p. 58)

14. A _____ Christian is what the Bible calls individuals who let his/her flesh be in charge. (p. 58)

15. Your body is supposed to be your _____, not your master. (p. 58)

16. The Bible tells us to bring our bodies into _____ and to present them as a living _____. (p. 58-59)

Life Application: Your Body

Use the concepts from chapter 4 to help you complete the following life application questions.

1. Do you struggle with maintaining control over your body? In what ways do you allow your body to be "in charge"?

2. How does it make you feel when you do not (or cannot) exert control over your body?

3. How do you currently take care of your body? (For example, do you jog? Eat fresh fruit and vegetables?)

4. How can you improve on caring for your body?

5. Most people have a hard time being content with their bodies, but each and every one of our bodies is a reflection of our Creator. What parts of your body are you grateful for and why? (For example, strong arms that help you hold your baby, sturdy legs that allow you to get through your hectic days, or even a loving heart to share with your family and with which to adore your Lord.)

6. Can you recall a time when your words caused damage?

7. How could you have prevented this damage?

8. List some ways you can use your speech to glorify God:

Chapter 5
YOUR ASSIGNMENT—YOUR GREAT ADVENTURE

Now that you have a better understanding of your spirit, soul, and body, it's time to discover God's plan for you. The following study questions will help you reflect on this great adventure.

Content Comprehension Questions
Refer back to chapter 5 to answer the following questions.

1. Your assignment is your _____. It's the reason you _____. (p. 61)

2. God creates every believer by _____ and with an _____. (p. 62)

3. God is _____ you, and _____ you and _____ you for your destiny. (p. 62)

4. God's plan for you is simply to be who He _____. (p. 62)

5. What does the author suggest to do to find out God's "assignment" for you? (p. 62)

6. Where can clues to your assignment be found? (p. 62-63)

7. As we learn to live out of our hearts, we find the courage to follow our _____ . (p. 63)

8. If we can get past fear, answers will come into _____ . Then we can walk with _____ . (p. 63)

9. Focus on your _____ , not your weaknesses. (p. 63)

10. **TRUE** or **FALSE**: We may be good at something, but not really enjoy it. (p. 63)

11. Listen to your heart (spirit) and begin to _____ . (p. 64)

12. It may take _____ to prepare you for your assignment. The important thing is that we're _____ after Him. (p. 65)

13. Following God's lead and staying focused on His will is called: _____ _____ _____ . (p. 65)

14. How will you know your destiny and be able to recognize it? (p. 65)

15. While some individuals may know from an early age what their destiny is, others may be led to their destiny as their life _____ . (p. 68)

16. God has a way of getting us where we're _____ to be. (p. 68)

17. Be open to the Lord's _____, and have the _____to follow that leading each day. (p. 68)

18. As you are obedient in the _____ things, the big picture will _____ _____ _____ _____. (p. 68)

19. Always remember: You are made with a _____and you are _____. (p. 68)

20. We all have _____ roles to play. (p. 68)

21. Never _____ the importance of your calling. (p. 68)

22. Everything God wants to do in the earth, He wants to do through _____ _____. (p. 68)

23. Your _____, your _____, and your _____ _____ are all found in your assignment. (p. 69)

24. You will effectively reach others through your own vital and living _____with the _____. (p. 69)

25. 2 Corinthians 5:20 tells us we are _____ for Christ. As you live out of your _____ with Him, this will come naturally and without effort. (p. 69)

26. Whatever you are _____ to do, you'll be truly _____ doing. Wherever your calling takes you is your _____ _____. (p. 69)

Life Application: Your Assignment
Use the concepts from chapter 5 to help you complete the following life application questions.

1. How do you think God will God show or reveal to you His plan for you?

2. To discover God's plan for you, you must focus on your strengths, not your weaknesses. List some of your strengths:

3. How can you further develop your strengths?

4. Kenneth Copeland Ministries tells us that we must obey "today…tomorrow…and the next day" to find out what God has planned for us. How can you focus more on obeying God?

5. Whatever God's plan is for you will make you truly happy. What are some things that currently make you happy?

6. In your quest to find your "assignment," how can you reach out to others with the Word of God?

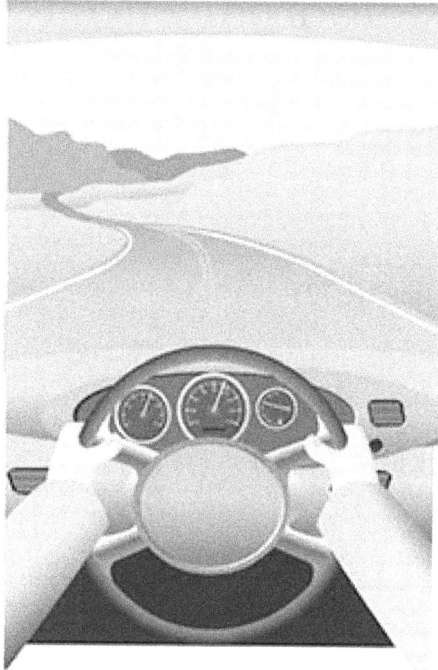

Chapter 6
JOURNEYING ON

Now that you have a better understanding of the different facets of your being and the uniqueness of your assignment, you can move forward toward your destiny with confidence and peace. The following study questions will help you review what you've learned and reflect on this great adventure and journey on with a sense of peace and contentment in simply being who God created.

Content Comprehension Questions
Refer back to chapter 6 to answer the following questions.

1. You are a complicated but _____, _____ _____ creation. (p. 71)

2. Psalm 139:14 says you are _____ and _____ made. (p. 71)

3. A better understanding of our three-part being brings us into a place of _____. (p. 71)

4. At salvation, we made the choice to _____ _____ as Savior. (p. 72)

5. This is also called the new _____. (p. 72)

6. During our _____ _____, we make daily choices to walk out our commitment to follow Him. (p. 72)

7. The more we learn about ourselves, the more we are _____ to live _____ in Christ. (p. 72)

8. We are _____, no longer to be controlled by _____ _____ or behave ourselves after a _____ _____. (p. 72)

9. Our _____ is our guide. (p. 72)

10. Living out of our _____ causes us not to be affected by what's happening in our other realms. (p. 72)

11. The voice in our spirit is often a "_____ certainty," while our soul and our flesh cry out with "_____ urges." (p. 72)

12. We make adjustments in our _____ and _____. (p. 73)

13. We take our thoughts _____ and renew our _____with the Word of God. (p. 73)

14. Our emotions _____ our living experience. They are _____ _____. (p. 73)

15. Our _____ is our right to choose the direction of our lives. (p. 73)

16. Our _____ is to serve us. (p. 73)

17. Who we are and what we have are _____ that God has given us, to equip us for _____ _____. (p. 73)

18. We find _____ in simply being who God _____. (p. 73)

19. Nourish yourself with things that will produce the _____ in your life that you _____. (p. 74)

20. You are a work in _____, and so is everybody else. (p. 74)

21. Phil 1:6 says God will complete the _____ _____ He began in you and bring it to _____. (p. 74)

All About Me

Life Application: Journeying On
Use the concepts from chapter 6 to help you complete the following life application questions.

1. After completing this book as well as the study guide, what have you learned about yourself that you did not know before?

2. List some ways you can nourish yourself in order to produce the results in your life you desire:

3. Illustrate how you feel your spirit, soul, and body are connected (use descriptive words, draw pictures, write a few lines of poetry—whatever helps you convey the image of your being):

46

NOTES

NOTES

NOTES

NOTES